POWERHOUSE

Inside a Nuclear Power Plant

POWERHOUSE

Inside a Nuclear Power Plant

by Charlotte Wilcox
photographs by Jerry Boucher

Carolrhoda Books, Inc./Minneapolis

Special thanks to Patrick Colgan, Ed Watzl, Donald Cragoe, Max Delong, Tom Boucher, and Cathy Gjermo for their assistance in the preparation of this book.

This book is available in two editions:
Library binding by Carolrhoda Books, Inc.
Soft cover by First Avenue Editions
c/o The Lerner Group
241 First Avenue North
Minneapolis, MN 55401

LIBRARY OF CONGRESS CATALOGING-IN-PUBLICATION DATA

Wilcox, Charlotte.
    Powerhouse : inside a nuclear power plant / by Charlotte Wilcox ; photographs by Jerry Boucher.
    p.   cm.
    Includes index.
    ISBN 0-87614-945-X (lib. bdg.)
    ISBN 0-87614-979-4 (pbk.)
    1. Nuclear power plants — Juvenile literature. [1. Nuclear power plants.] I. Boucher, Jerry, 1941–   ill. II. Title.
TK9148.W55   1995
621.48'3—dc20   95-9200
                                                      CIP
                                                       AC

Manufactured in the United States of America
1 2 3 4 5 6 – MP – 01 00 99 98 97 96

Metric Conversion Chart		
When You Know:	*Multiply by:*	*To Find:*
inches	2.54	centimeters
feet	0.30	meters
pounds	0.45	kilograms
tons	0.91	metric tons
cubic feet	0.03	cubic meters
degrees Fahrenheit	0.56 (after subtracting 32)	degrees Celsius

Contents

What Is Nuclear Power?

Have you ever wondered where your electricity comes from? You probably know that electricity travels in wires to your home and school. But where do the wires start? How does the electricity get into the wires in the first place?

What would your life be like without electricity?

Prairie Island nuclear power plant, on the Mississippi River in Minnesota

Electricity is made in large **power plants,** sometimes called powerhouses, which turn energy from natural resources into electricity. About half the electricity produced in the United States comes from coal. The second largest source is **nuclear energy,** which comes from a substance called **uranium.** Electricity made from nuclear energy is called **nuclear power.**

Some of your electricity may come from a nuclear power plant like the Prairie Island nuclear power plant near Minneapolis, Minnesota. Prairie Island is like most nuclear plants in North America, so a look inside this plant gives a good picture of how nuclear energy becomes electricity. Prairie Island started operating in 1973, but the history of nuclear power began much earlier.

Like many new inventions, making electricity from nuclear energy came from research done for a different purpose. In 1942, during World War II, scientists at the University of Chicago discovered how to unlock the tremendous energy inside tiny **atoms** of uranium. They hoped to end the war by making a weapon that could stop the military forces of Germany and Japan.

Three years later, American planes dropped atomic bombs on two cities in Japan. It is estimated that more than 100,000 people were killed instantly. The world was shocked by what this use of nuclear energy could do.

Efforts to use this new power to help people—not kill them—began after the war. Scientists soon found a way to use nuclear energy to make electricity in power plants.

The first nuclear power plant in the world was built near Arco, Idaho, in 1951. It was supplying the town's electricity by 1955. Large nuclear plants were soon making electricity in several countries. By 1990 there were over 100 nuclear plants in the United States and more than 400 worldwide. The energy produced in these plants was called nuclear power because it came from the **nucleus** of the atom.

On December 2, 1942, scientists at the University of Chicago succeeded in unlocking the tremendous energy inside atoms of uranium. Their work led to both the atomic bomb and the use of nuclear energy to make electricity.

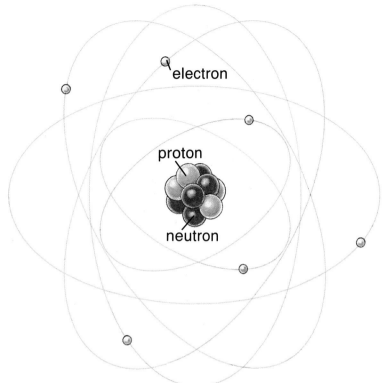

electron

proton

neutron

A Look inside an Atom

Atoms are the basic units of all matter and are too small to see, even with a microscope. Each atom is made up of even smaller particles—**protons, neutrons,** and **electrons.** Billions of atoms of the same kind group together to make **elements** that we observe in the natural world. Hydrogen, oxygen, and carbon are all common elements. They combine with about ninety other elements to form everything in our earth, water, and air.

An atom has a center, or nucleus, which contains its protons and neutrons. Electrons spin around the nucleus the way planets orbit the sun. Electrons stay in orbit because they have a negative electrical charge, while protons have a positive charge. Their opposite charges make protons and electrons act like magnets with each other. As long as the number of protons, neutrons, and electrons stays in balance, the atom holds together. But if the number of particles gets off balance, the atom splits apart.

To make electricity, this power plant burns 20,000 tons of coal every day.

Nuclear plants have some advantages over plants that use coal, oil, or natural gas. One is that nuclear plants use less natural resources. A nuclear plant doesn't burn anything the way a coal or oil plant does, so it doesn't pollute the air as much. Besides that, a coal plant releases about 100 times more **radiation** than a nuclear plant, because coal contains small amounts of uranium. But while nuclear power is a clean energy source, it is also very controversial.

 ACTUAL SIZE

One uranium fuel pellet
can produce as much electricity as:

1 ton of coal

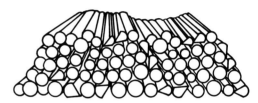

$2\frac{1}{2}$ tons of wood

3 barrels of oil   (126 gallons)

17,000 cubic feet of natural gas

Though nuclear power has many advantages, it uses and produces **radioactive** materials. These materials give off rays that can be harmful to living things, so the materials must be handled very carefully. They can remain dangerous for thousands of years—even after the useful energy they contain is used up.

Fire-fighting equipment is kept near an area where radioactive materials are used. Prairie Island has its own team of firefighters.

What Is Radiation?

The term radiation describes something moving in rays, or streams, of atomic particles. In order for atoms to hold together, they need just the right number of protons, neutrons, and electrons. If the number of particles gets off balance, an atom will throw off one or more particles to make itself stable again. Scientists call these atoms radioactive because they throw off rays as they try to stay in balance. Uranium and **plutonium** are two kinds of radioactive atoms.

About three-fourths of the radiation in the United States comes from the natural environment and is generally not considered harmful. Water, food, rocks, soil—even your own body—all give off small amounts of radiation. So do the sun and stars. You might encounter low levels of radiation from a smoke detector, a lighted clock, or cigarette smoke. About a fifth of the radiation you're likely to encounter in a lifetime will be in a medical clinic, dentist's office, or hospital—from X rays, scans, or medical treatments.

At high levels, radiation can kill or injure people, animals, and plants. Large amounts of radiation can contaminate soil, air, and water, which then pass the contamination on to any living creature that touches them.

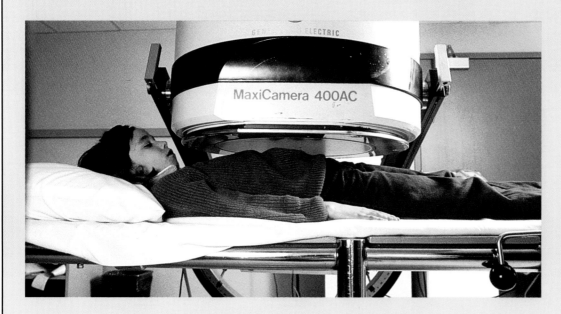

Doctors use radiation to scan part of a patient's body.

Even your TV set gives off a small amount of radiation.

No one in the United States has ever been exposed to a high level of radiation from a nuclear power plant. Tiny amounts of radiation—far less than what occur naturally in the environment—are released through air vents and in water that comes out of the plant. A family living one mile from a properly working nuclear plant would get twice as much radiation in a year from their television set. Over seventy years, they would absorb less radiation from the nuclear plant than they would from one chest X ray—as long as the power plant is operating properly.

Workers at Prairie Island are checked for radiation exposure every day. They press their bodies against a very sensitive radiation detector for about 20 seconds.

Fueling Nuclear Power

Most parts of the Prairie Island plant are no different from the parts of any power plant. Huge volumes of water flow in pipes through the plant—some boiling to make steam, some circulating to transfer heat and cool things down. Steam from the heated water rushes through a machine, making giant magnets spin to create electric **current.** The difference in a nuclear plant is the fuel that heats the water. The fuel that works in plants like Prairie Island is a kind of uranium called uranium-235.

Bulldozers mine uranium from the earth as **ore.** That ore contains less than 1 percent uranium—and only a small fraction of that is uranium-235. It takes a ton of ore to make five pounds of nuclear fuel!

Miners blast with dynamite to break up the rock that contains uranium ore.

People used to call uranium "yellowcake," after its bright yellow color.

Trucks haul the ore to a processing plant, where machines grind it to powder and remove the soil, leaving a higher concentration of uranium-235. Other machines shape tiny bits of uranium-235 into **fuel pellets.** Each pellet is about half an inch long and as big around as a piece of chalk.

Machines stack about 200 fuel pellets single file inside metal tubes, twelve feet long and as big around as an average man's finger. Then they group 179 filled tubes—called **fuel rods**—in a large bundle to form a **fuel assembly.** Trucks bring the completed assemblies to the nuclear power plant.

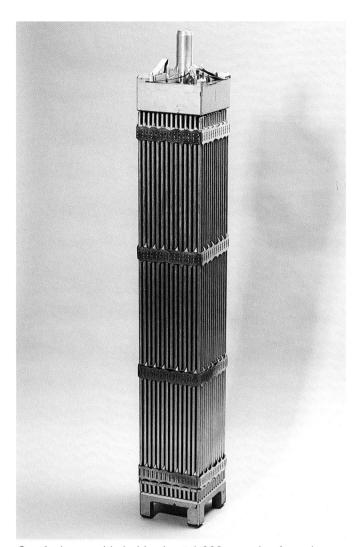

One fuel assembly holds about 1,000 pounds of uranium. It will not be highly radioactive until after it is used.

A uranium fuel pellet

The Reactor

At the nuclear power plant, workers load fuel assemblies into the **reactor.** A reactor is about the size of a school bus and has a thick steel shell around it. Prairie Island has two reactors, each housed inside a huge concrete and steel **containment building.** Each reactor is also surrounded by thousands of gallons of water and miles of pipes and wires.

A concrete wall, four feet thick and reinforced with steel, surrounds each of the two huge containment buildings at Prairie Island.

Inside the containment building, pipes and machines surround the reactor. In this picture, the reactor area looks blue because it is filled with water.

The Energy Cycle

All power plants generate electricity in the same way—by turning one kind of energy into another kind of energy that creates electric current. At Prairie Island, the energy goes through many changes before you can use it as electricity.

Nuclear energy . . .
Inside the reactor, splitting uranium atoms give off nuclear energy in the form of heat.

becomes thermal energy . . .
Water passing through the reactor gets very hot. It heats more water that boils and becomes steam.

becomes mechanical energy . . .
The steam turns blades attached to a long shaft.

becomes electrical energy.
The other end of the shaft is attached to magnets that spin to create electric current.

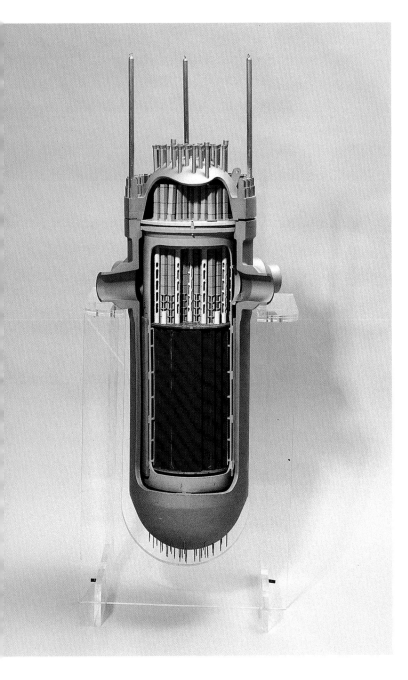

All of the equipment surrounding the reactor is designed to control **fission**—the splitting of uranium atoms. Fission takes place in the **core,** the center part of the reactor. Each Prairie Island reactor core holds 121 fuel assemblies, or sixty tons of uranium fuel.

Fission begins when a slow-moving neutron hits a uranium-235 atom. The neutron splits the atom into two new atoms. As it splits, the uranium atom gives off energy, mostly in the form of heat, and one or more neutrons. When many uranium atoms—billions of them—are close enough together, a neutron released from an atom has a good chance of splitting the nucleus of another atom and causing fission. A chain reaction occurs when many atoms continue splitting and splitting and splitting.

*The reactor is a sealed container, sort of like a thermos. This model shows what it looks like inside. The red area is the core, which contains the fuel assemblies. The gray shell around the reactor is the steel **reactor vessel**. The top of the reactor can be removed when workers need to put new fuel assemblies into the core.*

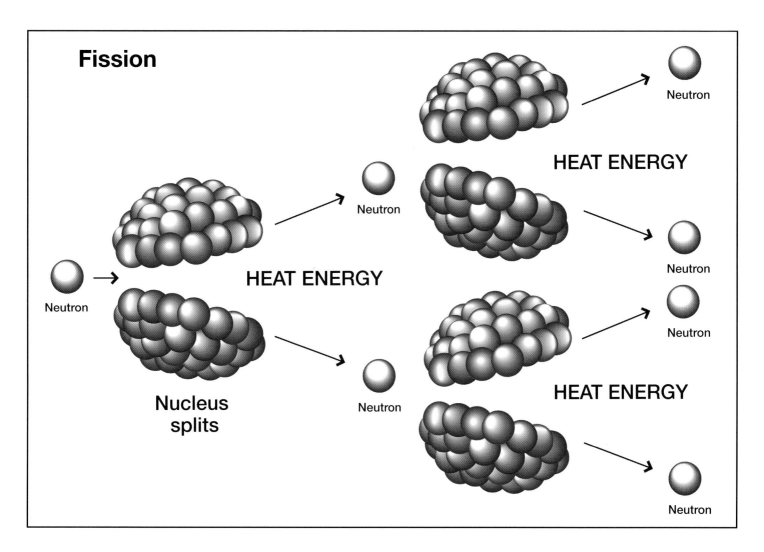

Fission

Neutron

Nucleus splits

HEAT ENERGY

Neutron

Neutron

HEAT ENERGY

Neutron

Neutron

HEAT ENERGY

Neutron

Neutron

Inside a brand-new fuel rod, there are plenty of uranium atoms close together, but the neutrons are moving too fast for fission to start. Fast-moving neutrons pass right through the nucleus without splitting it. Slow-moving neutrons are better at getting stuck in the nucleus and splitting it. Water must be added to slow the neutrons down before the fission process can start.

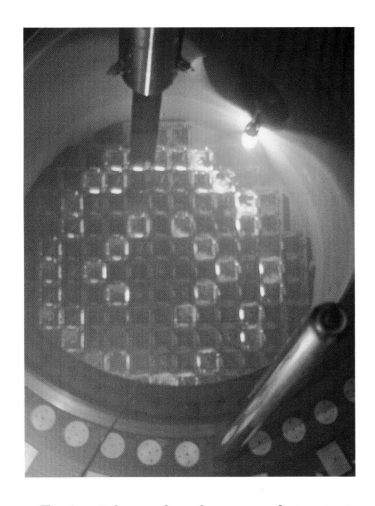

During refueling, fission is stopped. Workers use a crane (left) *to move fuel assemblies in the core. They also use a special detector* (below) *to make sure radiation levels are safe.*

Fission takes only a few seconds to start, and if properly controlled can continue for many months. Inside the reactor core, energy released by the fission of billions of atoms makes the fuel pellets get very hot—up to 2,500 degrees Fahrenheit. This heat is the first step in making electricity.

20

To help control the fission rate, workers at Prairie Island mix boron into the water that flows through the core. Boron absorbs moving neutrons. By adjusting the amount of boron in the water, operators can control how many neutrons are available to split other atoms. With water to keep fission going, and boron to slow it down when needed, operators can keep a steady chain reaction going.

A nuclear plant must be able to stop fission immediately if necessary. **Control rods** are made of silver, indium, and cadmium—materials that absorb neutrons very quickly. They are stored just above the fuel assemblies in the reactor. Each fuel assembly at Prairie Island has sixteen empty holes among the fuel rods. Control rods can be lowered into these holes. If all the control rods are lowered at once, they immediately begin absorbing neutrons and fission stops.

This model shows control rods lowered partway into a fuel assembly.

The Control Room

Workers at Prairie Island must carefully monitor everything that goes on in the plant around the clock. In the **control room,** several workers receive and analyze information from hundreds of places throughout the plant.

Prairie Island's control room

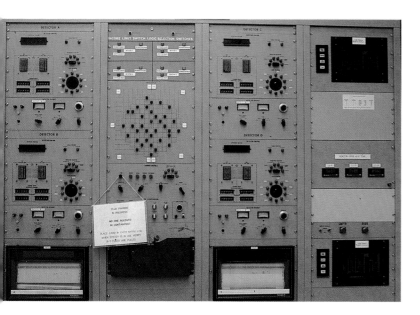

In the control room, some instruments (left) help workers keep track of what's happening inside the reactor. (Below) Workers can also check air flow in the containment building.

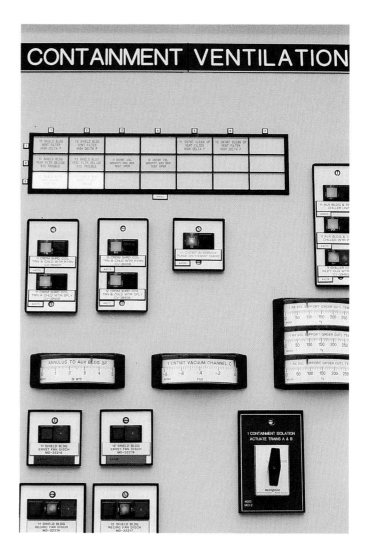

Some equipment in the control room measures and adjusts the delicate balance that keeps fission going safely inside the reactor core. The core is too radioactive for people to enter it—so electronic equipment sends information to hundreds of lights, screens, gauges, and dials in the control room. Other instruments receive information about the temperature, pressure, and flow of water throughout the plant.

About 400 workers run the rest of the equipment that the plant needs to control fission and to generate electricity. Once fission is under way, the next step is to heat the water.

Safety at Prairie Island

Because Prairie Island uses and produces materials that can be very dangerous, safety is an important part of the plant's operation. The number-one concern of workers in the control room and throughout the plant is keeping radioactivity inside the containment building.

The metal casing around the fuel rods, the steel reactor vessel, and the thick steel and concrete walls all keep radioactivity from getting out of the containment building. Special equipment controls the air pressure in the containment building so that it is less than the air pressure outdoors. This way, if any radioactive gases leak out of the core, they do not escape into the environment. The containment building is designed to automatically seal itself shut if an unsafe situation arises.

Plant supervisors meet here to decide how to handle emergencies.

Batteries (above) *serve as a backup power source in case of emergency. Inspectors from the Nuclear Regulatory Commission* (below right) *check the plant's safety.*

Another built-in safety feature is the water that flows around the fuel assemblies. If an area of fuel gets too hot, the water near it boils, making bubbles. Neutron movement speeds up where a hollow bubble forms. Fast-moving neutrons can't split as many atoms, so fission naturally slows down. Computerized sensors that measure the fission rate are built into the core. If they detect too much fission, they automatically shut down the reactor.

Emergency cooling systems come on automatically if the main cooling system stops working. Batteries and diesel generators are always on standby to provide emergency power for the safety systems if the plant loses its normal source of electricity.

Control-room workers at Prairie Island attend training classes one week out of every six weeks they work. Emergency drills show everyone what to do in case of a fire, natural disaster, or an accident in the plant. In training sessions with firefighters, police, and medical teams, plant workers learn how to handle emergencies.

In the United States, the Nuclear Regulatory Commission sees that nuclear plants meet safety standards. Government inspectors keep an office at Prairie Island and conduct inspections every day.

The Water Loops

The fission that takes place inside the reactor has one purpose—to heat water to make steam for generating electricity. Pumps circulate millions of gallons of water through three separate sets of pipes, called **water loops.** Each loop carries water in a circle that starts over once the water's job of transferring heat is done.

The primary loop carries water through the reactor core. The water gets very hot when it passes near the fissioning fuel. But the water in the primary loop does not boil because it is kept under pressure.

Miles of pipes carry water throughout the plant so the water can do its job of transferring heat.

How a Nuclear Power Plant Makes Electricity

This diagram shows how the water loops transfer heat energy. Water in the primary loop (red) is heated as it passes through the reactor core. Hot pipes of the primary loop heat water in the secondary loop (green), which then boils and turns to steam. The steam rushes through a turbine, which causes the generator to create electricity. The secondary loop then flows into the condenser, where cool water in the third loop (blue) turns the steam back into water.

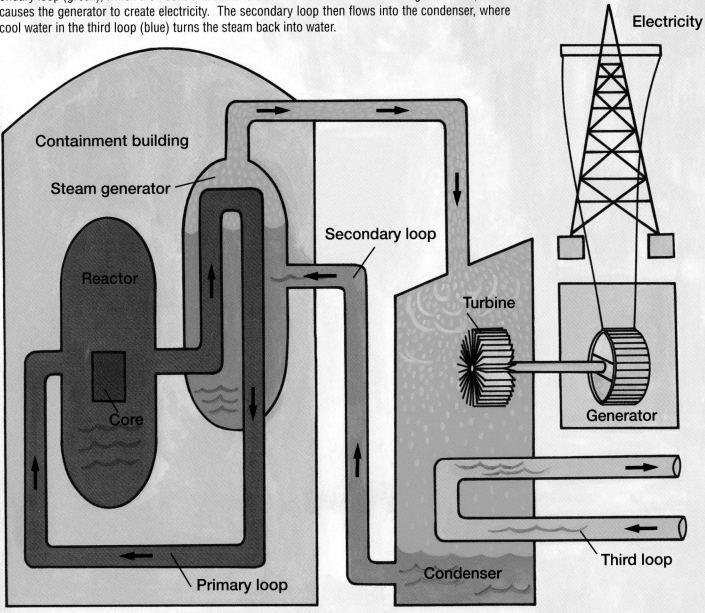

Electricity

Containment building

Steam generator

Reactor

Core

Secondary loop

Turbine

Generator

Primary loop

Condenser

Third loop

From the reactor core, the primary loop carries the heated water to the **steam generator,** where it flows into smaller pipes. At the same time, the secondary loop carries cooler water into the steam generator. Heat from the primary loop pipes is transferred to the secondary loop water. Water in the primary loop then flows back to the core to be heated again.

When the secondary loop flows into the steam generator, the water in the secondary loop gets hot and begins to boil. It turns to steam, just like water boiling on a stove. The power plant uses this steam to make electricity.

Water in the secondary loop travels to the steam generator (above), *where it becomes steam. Pipes of the secondary loop* (right) *carry the steam from the reactor area to the area where electricity is generated.*

Huge pipes in the third loop carry river water into the power plant.

After the steam has done its job, it must be turned back into water. Prairie Island's third loop brings cool water from a nearby river into a device called a **condenser.** The cool water absorbs the heat from the secondary loop's steam. This works in the same way that cold hands absorb the heat from a cup of hot cocoa. When you put cold hands on the cup, your hands get warmer and the cocoa gets cooler. When the steam in the secondary loop passes over the pipes of the third loop, water in the third loop gets warmer and the secondary loop gets cooler. The steam becomes water again. The secondary loop water then travels back toward the steam generator to begin another cycle.

Water vapor rises from cooling towers into the sky over Prairie Island.

The third loop carries its warm water to large outdoor tanks called **cooling towers.** Piped into the top of the towers, the water cools off as it falls through the air to the bottom of the towers. Then the cooled water flows back into the river.

Turning Heat into Electricity

During the time that the water in the secondary loop is hot enough to become steam, it runs through a **turbine.** A turbine is a cylinder-shaped machine that turns other forms of energy into electricity. The turbine has large blades, like the blades of a fan or propeller, attached to a long shaft. When rushing steam hits the turbine blades, they turn and make the shaft spin. The turbine acts like a windmill in the wind.

A spare turbine (above right) *is always kept on hand near the working turbine. Pipes carrying steam* (right) *lead into the top of the turbine shed. The rushing steam hits the blades of the turbine and makes them turn.*

From the turbine, the shaft reaches into the **generator,** where large magnets spin on the shaft as it turns. When the magnets spin, they create electric current in wires that are coiled inside the generator.

Part of the steel shaft can be seen between the turbine and the generator.

Magnets spin inside the generator, which is housed in the nearest rounded shed (left). *Below the generator, big bundles of wires, called "busses"* (below left), *carry electric current outside the plant.*

The energy that began inside tiny atoms too small to be seen has now become electricity that can travel to homes and businesses hundreds of miles away.

The Electric Highway

Electricity travels through wires from the generator to a **transformer** outside the plant. A transformer is a piece of equipment that changes the **voltage** (pressure or force) of electricity—from either a higher to a lower voltage, or the other way around. The transformer at Prairie Island increases voltage, giving the electricity an extra push so it can travel for hundreds of miles.

From the transformer, electric current passes along wires to the switchyard.

The transformer

From the switchyard, electric current goes out in many directions.

The current then flows through large cables to a switchyard near the plant. There the current is switched to power lines that branch out in all directions. Suspended on steel towers high above cities and farms, these lines carry electricity to neighborhood substations, which transform it to a lower voltage so it can go through smaller lines.

From a substation, smaller power lines take the current to small transformers located outside homes, buildings, and farms. These last transformers lower the voltage again to make it safe for the wiring in each particular building—so all you have to do is flick a switch when you want to turn on the light.

After a long journey, electricity can be used inside your home.

Nuclear Waste

At the same time that a nuclear power plant provides electricity for many homes, it also produces waste fuel. After about four and a half years in the reactor, a uranium fuel assembly has released most of its energy in the form of heat. Workers then take used fuel assemblies out of the reactor and replace them with new ones. At Prairie Island, workers carefully plan the use of fuel. In each of the two reactors, about forty fuel assemblies must be replaced every year and a half.

When used fuel comes out of the reactor, it is radioactive and still very hot. The fuel assemblies are put into a large pool of water, where they will cool for at least ten years. The older used fuel—what we call **nuclear waste**—is then put into special steel containers called **casks.**

The storage pool for used fuel at Prairie Island

A cask near Prairie Island is monitored twenty-four hours a day.

A cask is shaped like a large barrel, eight and a half feet across and as tall as a two-story building. Its walls are almost ten inches thick. Casks are tested to ensure that they can withstand fires, floods, earthquakes, tornadoes, and airplane and train crashes. Each cask costs about a million dollars.

Operators use a crane to lower a cask into the fuel storage pool. Then they place forty used fuel assemblies inside it and put on a heavy steel cover—all underwater. Next, they lift out the cask—which now weighs 122 tons—drain the water, seal the cask with large steel studs, and wash it to remove any radioactivity from the outside. The cask is warm to the touch but will cool over time.

Filled casks are placed on a heavy concrete floor outside the Prairie Island plant. Thick walls of earth, seventeen feet high, surround the floor.

Much care must be taken to store radioactive waste, even though a day's worth of waste from Prairie Island would not even fill a trash dumpster. That's not much compared to an average coal-burning plant, which hauls away 100 truckloads of ash every day! But because nuclear waste remains radioactive for thousands of years, how to store it safely is a big challenge.

All the nuclear fuel ever used by America's power plants could fit into a hole the size of one football field and about as deep as a two-story building—but right now it's not all in one place. It is stored all over the country, mostly at the power plants where it was used.

At first, all nuclear plants in the United States planned to send used fuel to recycling centers to be reprocessed into plutonium to fuel other reactors. But in 1982 Congress made it illegal to recycle nuclear fuel, because plutonium can also be made into atomic bombs. Instead, Congress decided to build a national storage plant for used fuel—but it won't be completed until the year 2010, at the earliest. Almost a third of the nuclear power plants in the United States will run out of storage space long before then.

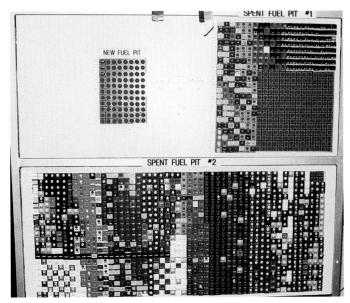

This grid shows where all of Prairie Island's fuel—both new and used—is stored.

The search for a good storage place has been going on since 1985. In 1987 Congress chose Yucca Mountain in Nevada. It has no active volcanoes, no recent history of earthquakes, and gets very little rain. The storage vault would be in a layer of dry rock almost a quarter of a mile under the mountain. However, many more tests are needed to see if it is really a good place. Besides that, the people of Nevada have not voted to allow radioactive waste storage there. A national storage site probably won't be ready anytime soon.

In the search for a national nuclear waste storage site, scientists must carefully study any area being considered. To learn more about the Yucca Mountain site, scientists conduct tests in this underground tunnel.

The Future of Nuclear Power

Many people in the nuclear power industry and in government agree that nuclear power plants cannot continue to operate for very many years without better ways to recycle or store used fuel. Besides that, many people question whether nuclear power's benefits—less air pollution, less use of natural resources—outweigh its challenges.

The people who put up this sign are concerned about the storage of nuclear waste near their homes.

Residents of San Luis Obispo, California, protest the Diablo Canyon nuclear power plant.

During the 1950s and 1960s, most people welcomed nuclear power as a clean energy source. But in the 1970s, people became more concerned about radiation and about terrorists stealing nuclear fuel to make bombs.

Two nuclear accidents also led many people to change their minds about nuclear power.

One accident in 1979, at the Three Mile Island nuclear plant in Pennsylvania, caused no health problems. But in 1986, a serious accident at Chernobyl, Ukraine, showed the public what can happen if nuclear fission gets out of control.

What Happened at Three Mile Island

On March 28, 1979, at the Three Mile Island nuclear power plant near Harrisburg, Pennsylvania, a valve in the primary loop stuck open and water escaped from a reactor. The emergency cooling system came on automatically—but operators shut it off by mistake. Before they realized it, the reactor core became too hot and melted some fuel rods. Some of the melted fuel dropped into the bottom of the reactor, which was full of water. The water stayed inside the reactor. There was no explosion, and no radioactive fuel escaped.

However, some radioactive air and water leaked through the open valve and escaped into the containment building. A small amount of radioactive gas was released into the environment. But the plant's safety features kept nearly all of the radiation inside the reactor, and no health problems resulted.

Three Mile Island nuclear power plant

What Happened at Chernobyl

On April 26, 1986, operators of a nuclear reactor at Chernobyl, Ukraine, made several mistakes that caused a buildup of neutrons in one area of the core. A fuel assembly soon shattered and began to melt.

Within minutes, gushing steam burst water pipes, blew off the roof, and destroyed the reactor building. In just a few hours, radioactive material shot three miles into the sky, spreading across the entire Northern Hemisphere. The reactor burned for ten days, until it was smothered with sand.

A reactor like the one at Chernobyl would not be allowed to operate in North America or Europe. The building that housed the Chernobyl reactor was not a steel and concrete containment building like those in North America, and the design of the reactor was very different.

At least thirty-one people died and hundreds were injured the first day. Radiation contaminated water and food thousands of miles away. More than 100,000 people around Chernobyl had to leave their homes, and some may not be able to return for decades. Thousands of people have since died from radiation poisoning.

On the fifth anniversary of the Chernobyl accident, Ukrainians protest continued use of the Chernobyl nuclear power plant.

Accidents and the difficulty of finding storage for used fuel have caused people around the world to question the future of nuclear power plants. No nuclear plants have been built in the United States since 1979.

However, people continue to use more and more electricity. Americans will probably need more than 200 new power plants by the year 2015. To help meet those energy needs and to ensure the future of nuclear power, scientists continue to develop safer and more efficient power plants.

Some scientists believe that future nuclear plants should have a new type of reactor, the **breeder reactor.** Reactors that use uranium-235, such as Prairie Island, convert only a fraction of their fuel into energy, but breeder reactors use plutonium, which is recycled from used uranium fuel. Breeder reactors are more efficient and produce less waste.

While scientific research continues, power companies and Congress are working on important decisions about nuclear waste storage and the future of nuclear power. Because the picture is constantly changing, everyone should stay informed about the benefits and the challenges of nuclear power.

The sun sets over the cooling towers at Prairie Island.

Glossary

atom: a basic unit of matter, made up of a nucleus of protons and neutrons surrounded by moving electrons

breeder reactor: a type of nuclear reactor that uses plutonium fuel and is very efficient

cask: a sealed steel container for storing used nuclear fuel

condenser: a device that cools steam, turning it back into water

containment building: the thick steel and concrete shell that surrounds a nuclear reactor

control rods: long rods that can move in and out of a reactor core to control fission by absorbing neutrons

control room: the area of a nuclear power plant where operators watch and control fission and other operations of the plant

cooling tower: an open water tank where warm water from the power plant is cooled by falling through the open air

core: the central part of a nuclear reactor where the fuel is located and where fission takes place

current: the flow of electricity through a wire

electrical energy: energy, produced as a result of magnetic force, which can be used to run machines

electron: a negatively charged particle that orbits the nucleus of an atom

element: any material that is made entirely of the same kind of atoms

fission: the chain reaction created when moving neutrons hit uranium atoms, causing them to split and release energy and particles

fuel assembly: a group of metal fuel rods filled with uranium fuel pellets

fuel pellet: a small piece of uranium-235, used to fuel nuclear reactors

fuel rod: the metal tube in which uranium fuel pellets are stacked

generator: a machine that converts mechanical energy into electrical energy by spinning magnets inside a wire coil

mechanical energy: energy released as a result of movement, such as the movement of parts of a machine

neutron: in the nucleus of an atom, a particle that carries no electrical charge

nuclear energy: energy released from the nucleus of an atom

nuclear power: electricity produced in a plant that uses energy from nuclear fission

nuclear waste: radioactive materials that are no longer useful, specifically used nuclear fuel

nucleus (plural, nuclei): the center of an atom, containing protons and neutrons

ore: soil or rocks from which valuable minerals can be separated out

plutonium: a radioactive element, rare in nature but produced inside a nuclear reactor

power plant: a place where electricity is generated

proton: in the nucleus of an atom, a particle that carries a positive electrical charge

radiation: rays, or streams, of particles thrown off by radioactive atoms

radioactive: the term used to describe materials that give off rays from their atoms

reactor: the container in which nuclear fission is started and controlled

reactor vessel: the steel structure that contains all parts of the reactor

steam generator: the device that transfers heat from hot water in the primary loop to cooler water in the secondary loop

thermal energy: energy created by raising the temperature of a substance

transformer: a device that increases or decreases the voltage of electric current

turbine: a machine with a central shaft, fitted with blades that turn from the pressure of water, steam, or gas

uranium: a naturally radioactive element, found in soil and rocks, used to fuel nuclear reactors

voltage: the force or pressure of electric current

water loop: a closed system of pipes that carries water in a circle, or loop, through a power plant

Index

Photo Credits
Additional photographs courtesy of: G.E. Nuclear
Energy, p. 8; © SIU/Visuals Unlimited, p. 12; TradeTech,
LLC, Denver, Colorado, p. 14 (both); Northern States
Power Company, pp. 17, 20 (both), 28 (left), 36; U.S.
Department of Energy, 39; © Roy David Farris/Visuals
Unlimited, p. 40; © Shmuel Thaler, p. 41; UPI/Bettmann,
p. 42; Reuters/Bettmann, p. 43.